RETURN TO THE FATHER

By the same author

David: Sinner and Believer
The Dove at Rest
The Gifts of the Holy Spirit
Promise Fulfilled
What Am I That You Care for Me? – Praying with the Psalms
The Woman Among Her People

CARLO MARIA MARTINI

Return to the Father

"I will get up and go back to my Father"
(Lk 15:18)

Translated by Stephen Connolly

ST PAULS

Original title: *Ritorno al Padre di tutti*

Translated from Italian

Copyright © 1998 ITL spa, Milano, Italy

ST PAULS Publishing
Morpeth Terrace, London SW1P 1EP, U.K.

Copyright (English Translation) © ST PAULS 1999

ISBN 085439 563 6

Set by TuKan, High Wycombe
Produced in the EC
Printed by The Guernsey Press Co. Ltd., Guernsey, C.I.

ST PAULS is an activity of the priests and brothers of
the Society of St Paul who proclaim the Gospel
through the media of social communication

Contents

A brief dialogue with Paul VI   7
The Parable of the Merciful Father   10
Introduction   13

I   **Let us go to the Father**   17
    1. The ways of personal disquiet:
       'I will get up and go to my father'   17
    2. The ways of disquiet of an era:
       secularism and the fatherless society   22
    3. Life as a pilgrimage towards the Father   27

II   **Let us listen to the Father's revelation**   31
    4. The Father of Israel   31
    5. Abba, the Father of Jesus   35
    6. The Father of the disciples, 'Our Father'   37

III **Let us meet one another in the Father of us all!**   43
    7. With those who believe in God   43
    8. With those who do not believe (those who
       are searching and the indifferent)   48
    9. With the poor   53

In praise of the Father: the image of Mary   57
Appendix   61

A brief dialogue with Paul VI*

PAUL VI: What theme are you thinking of choosing for this year's pastoral letter (1998-99)? What will you suggest for the diocese which was my own for over eight years (1954-1963)?

ME: Naturally I am choosing the theme of "God the Father" since your successor John Paul II has chosen it for the third year of preparation for the Millennium.

PAUL VI: That's the same one as I chose for the great mission of Milan in 1957 when I was Archbishop! I was so fond of this theme. As I said to the priests gathered at Milan on the 22nd of October of that year, I wanted in this way to draw attention to the "essential relationships and the fundamental truths of our religion", to search out "the foundations of our dealings with God".

ME: This discussion of the fundamentals is giving me a lot of trouble, as a matter of fact. I am

---

* Giovanni Battista Montini, with whom Cardinal Martini holds this imaginary dialogue, was elected Pope in June 1963, taking the name Paul VI. He helped guide the Church through the transformation (still in process) it underwent as a result of the Second Vatican Council. Before being elected Pope he had been Archbishop of the Milan Diocese, as Cardinal Martini is now.

worried I might write a letter which is too abstract, too conceptual, and the work is becoming quite lengthy. God as "Father" is at the root of everything, from him "all fatherhood in heaven and on earth takes its name." (Eph 3:15). What should I concentrate on?

PAUL VI: I felt worried at taking on a theme so much bigger than I am as well. Don't worry, though: entrust yourself to the Father's providence. He feeds the birds of heaven and the lilies of the field and has counted the hairs on your head. I'll give you some advice: Let yourself be inspired by the parable of the "prodigal son and the merciful father" in Luke's Gospel. It is the parable of a modern society that has lost its sense of who the Father truly is.

ME: Ah, modern men and women! You were always so conscious of this demanding and elusive questioner. However, I find another difficulty here. They say that ours is a society without a father (A. Mitscherlich), so how will it listen to a discourse about the fatherhood of God? I can already feel a flood of objections and criticisms building up...

PAUL VI: "You are worried and distracted by many things" (Lk 10:41). Trust in the Holy Spirit and in the minds and hearts of your readers. "No one knows the Father except the Son and anyone to whom the Son chooses to reveal him." (Mt 11:27). Give expression to what you feel inside, without worrying. And don't try to say everything there is to say. The Spirit, the interior Teacher, will fulfil his role, which is the most important one.

Moreover, I have confidence in our Ambrosian parishes. I am sure that at the outset of the pastoral year they will make some time for contemplative quiet so they can grasp the spirit of your letter.

ME: Thank you for your encouragement. I needed it. But you should also pray to the Father for me, in this the centenary year of your birth and baptism (1897) and twenty years after your death (1978), so it may be granted me to do the little I can and that God expects of me. Pray, too, for those who come across these pages. Ask that they should know how to re-read Luke's parable with me so as to enter a little more into the Father's heart.

The Parable of
the Merciful Father

Then Jesus said, "There was a man who had two sons. The younger of them said to his father, 'Father, give me the share of the property that will belong to me.' So he divided his property between them.

"A few days later the younger son gathered all he had and travelled to a distant country, and there he squandered his property in dissolute living. When he had spent everything, a severe famine took place throughout that country, and he began to be in need. So he went and hired himself out to one of the citizens of that country, who sent him to his fields to feed the pigs. He would gladly have filled himself with the pods that the pigs were eating; and no one gave him anything.

"But when he came to himself he said, 'How many of my father's hired hands have bread enough and to spare, but here I am dying of hunger! I will get up and go to my father, and I will say to him, "Father, I have sinned against heaven and before you; I am no longer worthy to be called your son; treat me like one of your hired hands.' So he set off and went to his father.

But while he was still far off, his father saw him and was filled with compassion; he ran and put his arms around him and kissed him.

Then the son said to him, 'Father, I have sinned against heaven and before you; I am no longer worthy to be called your son.' But the father said to his slaves, 'Quickly, bring out a robe – the best one – and put it on him; put a ring on his finger and sandals on his feet. And get the fatted calf and kill it, and let us eat and celebrate; for this son of mine was dead and is alive again; he was lost and is found!' And they began to celebrate.

"Now his elder son was in the field; and when he came and approached the house, he heard music and dancing. He called one of the slaves and asked what was going on. He replied, "Your brother has come, and your father has killed the fatted calf, because he has got him back safe and sound.' Then he became angry and refused to go in.

"His father came out and began to plead with him. But he answered his father, 'Listen! For all these years I have been working like a slave for you, and I have never disobeyed your command; yet you have never given me even a young goat so that I might celebrate with my friends. But when this son of yours came back, who has devoured your property with prostitutes, you killed the fatted calf for him!' Then the father said to him, 'Son, you are always with me, and all that is mine is yours. But we had to celebrate and rejoice, because this brother of yours was dead and has come to life; he was lost and has been found.'"

Introduction

This year I am going to speak about God the Father, the Father of Jesus Christ and of us all. The theme was suggested by John Paul II, who, after asking us to speak of Jesus (cf *I Speak to your Heart,* Pastoral Letter of the Milan Diocese 1997) and of the Holy Spirit (cf *Three Tales of the Spirit,* Pastoral Letter of the Milan Diocese 1998), now asks us to dedicate this last year before 2000 to the Father. It is also the theme which, as you will have noted in the previous dialogue with Paul VI, this great pope chose for the great mission of Milan when he was our archbishop.

It might seem a rather obvious theme for a Christian baptised in the name of the Father and of the Son and of the Holy Spirit, quite used since childhood to beginning the sign of the Cross "in the name of the Father". However I have perceived in some surveys a certain resistance to using the name "Father" when referring to God. There is still a feeling in the air that the father figure has been rejected. Quite a few people refer to disappointing experiences of human fatherhood that would not allow them to apply that name comfortably to the One who ought never to be a disappointment to us. Others have asked themselves, "Why not talk of God using the word 'mother', at least as often as we use 'father'."

The crowding of diverse and contradictory feelings towards the father figure has convinced me that this is not an easy matter to talk about. I realise that I will have to burrow under the surface of our everyday lives and modern culture in order to clarify things and discover the right way to say to God, "Father, my Father!" Who will have the courage to follow me? Who will have the strength not to lazily resign themselves to the duplicity and contradictoriness of their reactions towards God, that leave them one minute wanting to be cuddled like a baby in their father (or mother's) arms, the next minute wanting to distance themselves like a youth in search of freedom and independence?

Reflecting on these things I realise that it has never been obvious, not even in the past, how to accept a father figure easily. Jesus told us this in the parable of the two sons that I recalled at the beginning of this letter (Lk 15:11-32). Neither of the two was able to live out the truth of his relationship with his father. Both of them rejected it in one way or another. It took a long journey for the younger son to truly meet his father, whereas we do not know even today whether the elder made the journey himself. What is clear from the parable is that God is truly father (and mother) to us all; that it is difficult for all of us to recognise God as such; and that no-one can discover their true identity until they have returned to the Father.

My letter is therefore about how difficult it is to recognise the father, how bitter is our, and our modern culture's, rejection of the Father, and how certain it is that life has meaning only when we see it as a return to the Father: "Let us go to the Father!". This is the first part of the letter.

In the second part ("Let us listen to the Father's revelation!"), we will see how it is God who shows us the paths towards God and how God clears the way for us.

In the third part ("Let us meet one another in the Father of us all!") we will look at what this journey means for all of us, fellow-travellers, often preoccupied by our confessional, religious, racial and social differences, but in fact all on a pilgrimage towards one single goal.

What are my hopes for this letter? Above all I would like it to be read as a *vade mecum*; that no-one be frightened off by a tough beginning; that at the end, we are able to say "Father" in a similar way that Jesus did, with words and actions worthy of a rediscovered brotherhood and sisterhood before the only Father.

I foresee two possible kinds of indolent pilgrims on this journey towards the Father: some believers who say, "I know quite well who my Father in heaven is, and this letter will have nothing new to say to me," and others, non-believers, who think, "it's just the same old stuff and I'm not interested." In fact these two resistances are present in whoever is reading this now, and in me who is writing it. There is something of the first and of the second son in each of us: we believe we know the Father, but in fact we only know him from a distance. There is therefore a discovery to be made. I wish that everyone were able to make it, beginning with myself; and of course, as Pope Montini reminded me above, it is thanks especially to the "interior Teacher" that we can. I know it is quite a difficult road. Nevertheless, without it I fear that the "Year of the Father" will end up as a heap of pious phrases without having inspired any true conversion of heart. What sense would there be in celebrating a Jubilee like that? What would be the point of celebrating the two thousand years since the birth of Christ without making the effort to enter into the mystery of his divine sonship and of our sharing in his life?

I

Let us go to the Father

1. The ways of personal disquiet: "I will get up and go to my father" (Lk 15:18)

There are many ways to reject the Father and the road that leads towards him. The most common (and the most hidden from our unconscious) is the denial of death. Nevertheless, all of us, without exception, are on a journey, whether long or short, that will inexorably lead to it. To live is to co-exist with the notion that sooner or later everything will come to an end. There are some who console themselves with the idea that when death overtakes us we will no longer exist, and that as long as we exist, there is no death. This is a poor consolation. In reality death overshadows every instant of our lives in the form of a question: What will become of me after I die? What meaning does life have for me? Where am I going with all this burden of effort, pain and scant consolation?

Death seems, in these questions, like a radical challenge to human thinking, a challenge which demands serious reflection from us all. It is like a sentinel watching over the mystery, like the hard rock that keeps us from sinking into superficiality. It is a signal we cannot escape from, that constrains us to seek after a goal worth living for. It's the "final frontier" (E. Montale) from which, like a rebound, the urge springs up in us to fight against the apparent triumph of death and the deep need to seek for a meaning in life, to justify the struggles of every day.

I feel that when they read these words some people will be tempted to reject them: why begin with such a serious matter so devoid of the hope that comes from Scripture? However, I have only recalled the events narrated by Jesus in the parable of the two sons. It is when the younger son, who asked to leave his father's house and squandered his riches, finds himself at rock bottom ("He would gladly have filled himself with the pods that the pigs were eating; and no one gave him anything." Lk 15:16) that, almost by rebound he remembers that his father has a house where the servants have a life, dignity and "bread enough and to spare" (Lk 15:17). The experience of destitution permits him to look without fear at the road he was travelling on towards his death and to turn his back on it. When we feel lonely, when no-one seems to like us any more and we have our own reasons for hating or being unhappy with ourselves, when the prospect of death or grave loss scares us and casts us into depression, that is when, from the depths of out heart, the presentiment of, and longing for, an Other wells up in our hearts – someone who can welcome us and make us feel loved, above and beyond anything and in spite of everything else.

In this sense the Father – if a more worldly and secular sense were required – is the image of someone to whom we can entrust ourselves unreservedly, the harbour where all our exhaustion finds its rest, secure that we will not be rejected. This father figure has at once fatherly and motherly traits: we can talk of him as the Father in whose arms we feel safe and as a Mother whom we acknowledge as the source of life. For this reason the Father calls to mind the beginnings, the womb, our homeland, house and hearth, a heart to whom we entrust all that we are, a face to gaze upon without fear. The need for the Father can therefore be compared to the need for a reference point and a fatherly and motherly refuge; it can be given expression using either male or female images without distinction.

In this light the words of the prodigal son, *"I will get up and go to my father"* gives voice to the need for an origin we can recognise as our own beginning, for companions who make us feel loved and forgiven, for a goal to aim towards. The fundamental anxiety of being on the road to death, as if flung towards it; and the homesickness for a Father-Mother to call upon to save us: these are two aspects of a single process that takes place in our hearts, even though it can be less than dramatic, working itself out in the small hopes and fears of every day. In as much as we are all filled, to a greater or lesser extent, with anxiety, we are all journeying towards the Father, fired by the homesickness for our mother's and father's home where we will discover the certainty that we are understood and welcomed.

If this is the situation, why do so many show an almost visceral rejection of the father-figure? Why is the Father-Mother of our origins also for many an adversary to be fought, the opposition from whom we must flee and be delivered? Why did the youngest son of the parable want to "go away" from his father and his father's house?

The reasons why the prodigal wanted to leave home are the same reasons behind the coining of the word 'patricide'. The word denotes the impulse we have within us to ask for reasons and explanations from the person we be believe is in some way above us, to ask for what we believe is our due so we can finally be masters of ourselves and our fate, to make "what we want" of ourselves. However, to do that we have to erase the father figure in some way, behave as if he no longer existed, and suppress him. One voice among many bears witness to this rejection: "The feeling of nothingness that often overcomes me," wrote Franz Kafka in his *Letter to My Father* in November 1919, "owes its beginnings mainly to your influence... I could only taste what you gave us at the expense of shame, struggle, weakness and feelings of guilt. I could only give you recognition in the same way a beggar would, but not as things actually were. The main result of this education was to make me flee from anything that reminded me of you, however remotely."

The rejection of the father by so many of our contemporaries makes us wary of using the father figure (and to a certain extent the mother figure as well) to excess when we speak of God. Whenever we talk of "returning to the Father" we don't mean some kind of regression to childish dependence, nor the deep conflict that it might evoke in some people. The Father-Mother we are speaking about here is a metaphor for the mysterious and ultimate Other we can entrust ourselves to without fear, certain that we will be welcomed, cleansed and forgiven. Many of us have had a glimpse of the face of a Father-Mother who is able to love us unreservedly, in the happy experiences of our relationships with our own fathers and mothers. But there are some whose experiences were not entirely happy, and still others for whom the experience was negative, who may perhaps feel in their hearts an even stronger yearning for the utterly Other they can abandon themselves to.

The Other who offers itself to each of us in love as a Father-Mother, as a merciful and faithful "Thou" is the Other revealed to us by Jesus. This is not an aspiration, a wish or some vain inward hope. It is real, it has been made known to us, and we can be sure of it like a foundation stone, like arms holding us tight, like a heart that beats for us. We will talk about it in the second part of our letter.

It is certainly legitimate for us to bring to our encounter with the Father all our worries, weaknesses and fears (this is where we began), with the hope and expectation they bring of the Other. The revelation of God the Father meets our fears and expectations; but it does not flow from them, it precedes them and has its own incontrovertible, historical truth. Providentially, God comes to meet us and gives meaning to the return, the rediscovery of the Father that is the journey of every man and woman on earth.

2. The ways of disquiet of an era: secularism and the fatherless society

The process by which individuals have become estranged from their fathers, which we have so far only outlined, has also taken place on a collective level, in common mindsets, during the most recent centuries of our history, and has given birth to the current atmosphere of secularism. The Enlightenment of the eighteenth century wanted, as we know, to usher in an age of adult thought, self-mastery and mastery of the world's future, where everyone would be able to look after themselves and organise their lives in accord with their own plans and projects.

This ambition of the modern age, which has inspired the major revolutions, has evinced its deep ambiguity more and more. On the one hand grown-up thought has demanded the explanation of everything and produced the great generalising ideologies. This has led to the forceful elimination of all that might seem different (of a different faith, social condition, race or nation – which has led to police states, death camps, ethnic cleansing, and so on). On the other hand, as if by counter-reaction, the systematic denial of any dependence upon Someone above has led to a seeking after idols, that is, mere "Father substitutes" which bear the face of their charismatic leader or party, the idea of 'progress', and so forth.

This process has dramatically resulted in the explicit denial of God, understood as Father and Lord. In this way a systematic atheism has developed, the corollary of the struggle for complete emancipation. In consequence, the "death of God" is seen as a necessary prerequisite of humanity's life and glory. There is the desire to be free of a God who is understood as a despotic judge, or indifferent or inert opponent.

The tragic cost of these demands of modern reason soon became apparent. Two analysts of our age began their study with the following words: "The Enlightenment, understood in its widest sense as thought in constant progress, has always pursued the goal of freeing people from fear and making them masters. But our completely enlightened world glitters with the victorious standards of misfortune triumphant (Max Horkheimer and Th. W. Adorno, *Enlightenment Dialectic*). Enlightenment ideology has been overturned in the smoke of the cremation ovens and in the genocides committed this century. The fatherless society produced by Reason's totalitarian ambitions has resolved itself into a crowd of solitudes. The so-called "ideological crisis" and the development of "weak thought", which characterise the end of the millennium, hide the failure experienced by the demands of grown-up Reason.

What does this mean in real terms? It means that the bold frontiers of common sense are crumbling, that there is an increasing rejection of ideological certainties, and that there is a growing sense of unease and rootlessness. Our age of opposing ideological blocs could be described as "a shipwreck with a spectator" (H. Blumenberg). Indifference, the lack of any passion for truth and the

23

inability to hope for anything of consequence spurs many to close themselves within the narrow horizons of their own needs or those of their group. Fragmentation has taken the place of organic systems. The archipelago has become a substitute for enforced ideological collectivism. "Weak thought", wary of any truth, gains the upper hand.

What becomes of the father in this post-modern situation? If ideology had wanted to liberate humanity from dependence on the father in the hope of making us into free adults, the "weak thought" that has taken its place fails to restore to us the Other we can entrust ourselves to. The end of the society without fathers does not mean the return to the father figure. In fact the relativism which spread as a consequence of the abandonment of ideological certainty would appear to have made us even more closed up in ourselves and more alone. Indifference to values, often hidden behind the mask of ambition and a wild existence frittered away on trifles, has taken a more radical step towards the "murder of the father" committed by Enlightenment reason. The father is now no longer an adversary to be fought against or a despot to be freed from, but has become a figure deprived of any interest or attraction. And to ignore the father is even more tragic than to fight against him in the hope of freedom.

Relativism and indifference thus have an effect on our experience of God as Father: "weak thought" doesn't deny God, nor does it feel the need to do so, but it empties the transcendent of all meaning and attraction. At worst God becomes a kind of "ornament" (G. Vattimo), a figure who compromises himself with moral weakness and continual falling into absurdity: God becomes weak, the mirror of a decadent and yielding humanity. We live with God as if with one of the many fetishes around us without permitting ourselves in any way to become marked or transformed by God: we are like the elder son in the parable of the merciful father (Lk 15:11-32), who stayed at home but who, after so many years living with his father, is still unable to grasp the logic of his love and forgiveness. The elder son was a prisoner of his own loneliness and a slave of his own interests ("you have never given me even a young goat!" Lk 15:29), and he is no less distant from the father than the other son who had left home – physical proximity is not the same as closeness of the heart. You can live in the father's house yet ignore him in your actions. You can keep on speaking of God but fail to meet God or have any deep and life-giving experience of God.

Thus far I have attempted an explanation of what happens after the "rejection of the Father" that results from secularism and "weak thought". But what do we see of all this in the people we deal with every day? Obviously we don't often come across this situation lived out in an organised and logical fashion. Without noticing it, ordinary people live in very different cultural milieux. In part they are aware deep down of a fatherhood that comes from above and they pray the *Our Father*, at least occasionally, with trustfulness. In part they unconsciously share our modern culture's diffidence towards the father and would like to free themselves from a God who seems like a kind of father-master. They are also open to postmodernity's bewildering influences, which are expressed not so much in terms of systems and logic, but through a general sense of indifference, apathy, mistrust of higher truths, and a drift towards the more ephemeral. It is this latter aspect that explains the distance many middle-aged people have put between themselves and the Church, as well as the indifference and lack of purpose in so many of our young people.

I would like those who are reading this to make a further step, to look inside themselves and re-read as part of their own interior framework the co-ordinates we have examined, not just as a part of the cultural history of the last three centuries. The parable of the two sons (Lk 15) makes this demand of us – to enter into those two characters and say to ourselves "You are that person" (cf 2 Sam 12:7). It is only when we experience in ourselves the flotsam and jetsam of our own times, taking note of the good and bad points, that we will be able to stop looking at those around us who struggle with their Christian faith and life as outsiders, feeling uneasily and haughtily distant from them. We will be able to treat them as fellow-travellers, part of our own history, mirrors of our own interior life, and we will tell them and ourselves the words of truth the Spirit speaks to us inside. In fact the Spirit of Jesus says "Abba, Father" in us, men and women of an indifferent and distracted postmodernity. Whoever can discern the voice of the Spirit is called to help others to listen to this voice, so that it may shout even today in the hearts of each one of us.

3. Life as a pilgrimage towards the Father

How can we help others to perceive the voice of the Spirit? How can we uncover the Father's face as a true, attractive face? How can we restore to our age the taste for an ultimate, mysterious and loving point of reference, for an original womb in which we can move and act, enabled to make sense of our lives?

The twofold analysis I have sketched out – one that moves lovingly from the dread of living in isolation towards the Father-Mother, and one that reads in the advent of secularism the rejection of the father figure and a lapse into indifference – demonstrates the inevitability of our choice. Wherever we close in upon ourselves or try to encompass the entire universe in the narrow horizon of our personal goals, then dread, absurdity and loneliness prevail. But whenever we try to remain open to discovery and broaden our horizons, the father figure comes to meet us, calling us by name.

So we are invited to view our lives and our history as a pilgrimage towards the Father: we live not for death but for life and this final destination is linked to Someone who comes to meet us and guarantees our future as a pact and covenant with him. Whenever we open ourselves to the Other who visits us and helps us come out of our fears and selfishness so as to live for and with others, peace accords are forged and conversations are born that were formerly held to be impossible. Our existence is a road towards the promised land that comes to meet us like some holy Mystery we entrust ourselves to and let ourselves be met and saved by.

The loving Father-Mother figure appears here in all its newness when compared to all the false images we have so often made of it: it is not in competition with humanity, with our freedom and our work of liberation. The image of the despotic father we want to be free of is often projected onto God. It should be rejected, but not with the aim of promoting an absolute emancipation that might – as has happened in systematic ideologies – bring in through the window what was chased out of the door, filling our lives and our histories with new dependencies worse than the earlier ones. We need to go back to the Father who makes us free and calls us to freedom, to the one who spurs us to become ourselves and build our future responsibly and who builds the future with us. It is a question of thinking of the Father in accordance with the parable of mercy: the father respects the younger son's freedom, even to the point of suffering with love and expectation; he hopes the son will return and is happy when this longed-for return comes about, without however having ever tried to force the boy's decisions; he is quick to forgive and welcome his son back to a new life without recrimination or regrets.

At this point, at the end of this first part of the letter in which I have tried to put in focus the difficulties we have these days when we try to speak of God as a "Father", we could begin to reflect on the theme of human fatherhood and motherhood, in particular on the mistaken ways of being a father or a mother.

If the knowledge of God as Father is not merely

a projection of our own experience of calling some-one on earth "Father" and "Mother", but rather a revelation from above, as we shall see at length in the second part of our letter, it is no less true that every bad experience that we have in the bosom of the family runs the risk of darkening the fatherly image of God, burdening it with the bitterness and lost opportunities that scar many of us in child-hood and adolescence. We might say the same of every kind of relationship that corresponds in some way to "fatherhood": pastoral relationships, like that of pastors in dealings with their people, or spiritual ones, such as directing others in the ways of faith and discernment.

Bearing in mind what has already been said, it could be possible to outline some kind of distorted typology of fatherhood and motherhood, just as it is possible to outline, in the mystery of God's father-hood, guidelines for overcoming it. It is a matter of rethinking the role of parents within the family (and all similar relationships) in the light of the mysterious relationship of fatherhood and sonship between God and humanity. Think for example of how in modern society we confuse the "merciful father" with the indulgent father, who doesn't know how to teach his children to bear life's burdens. Then on the contrary there is the call for fatherly authority that is twisted into the idea of a father-master.

It is enough for me to have mentioned this idea, as we can take it up again during the year. It is important now to return to the substance of the Gospel parable, the "merciful father" that teaches us the right kind of attitude for our return to the Father.

"*I will get up and go to my father*" – the path of our liberation and the overcoming of the crisis of secularism hinges on this decision to become pilgrims and go out to meet the welcoming embrace of the Other.

To *get up and go* means not allowing homesickness for an existence lived entirely in our minds to get the better of us, nor allowing ourselves to be seduced by the lure of a present in which we can rest in our small certainties or lamenting our failures.

To *get up and go* means accepting that we will always be searching, listening for the Other, reaching out towards a meeting that will surprise and change us, when we will finally be willing to obey in a mature way (cf Mt 21:28-31 – the parable of the two sons).

To *get up and go* means to begin living again in hope, with hopes. "We are poor beggars, this is the truth": this saying, attributed to the dying Luther, is not only the honest confession of one who has met his own limitations, but also the declaration of a life-project that is searching outside itself in the Other, in the Father-Mother, in love, for a meaning in life and in history. So let us go together to the Father and listen to his Word, in whom he has told us of himself.

II

Let us listen
to the Father's revelation

4. The Father of Israel

The parable of the return of the son in Luke 15 presents us with a face of God that is in deep continuity with the God of Israelite faith.

The idea of "return" underlies the Hebrew word *shuv*, which means "conversion", the change of heart and life, and includes the idea of "going back", retracing the steps of a mistaken journey.

In the parable the father assumes the most original features of the Jewish faith's God: he is humble, because he respects the son's decisions even when it hurts. The God of Israel so loves his people and respects their decisions that he "contradicts" himself in order to make room for his beloved creature's freedom.

Divine humility is conjoined to the suffering love of this father: even the God of the promise cannot remain unmoved when confronted by the behaviour of his people and he suffers when they are unfaithful. God's love is not only an expression of *hesed*, strong, tenacious and faithful when put to the test, but also of *rachamim*, maternal, deeply felt love for one's own children. "But Zion said, 'The Lord has forsaken me, my Lord has forgotten *me.*' Can a woman forget her nursing child, or show no compassion for the child of her womb? Even these may forget, yet I will not forget you. See, I have inscribed you on the palms of my hands; your walls are continually before me." (Is 49:14-16)

Reading between the lines in the parable there is a strong sense that the son's return is almost necessary for the father to be who he is. How could he live without his son, when he spends every day looking out at the horizon ready to jump for joy and meet him when he returns? (cf Lk 15:20). At any rate, God's love for us is so great that he has chosen to be nothing if not with us: the name God chose for himself for all time is "God-with-us" (cf Mt 1:23; Apoc 21:3).

The Father of Israel is also Mother, the Other to whom we can entrust ourselves utterly, a God faithful to love's promises, the rock on which to build a life, secure that we will not be disappointed. John Paul II wrote in the encyclical *Dives in Misericordia*, "The Old Testament proclaims the mercy of the Lord by the use of many terms with related meanings; they are differentiated by their particular content, but *it could be said that they all converge from different directions on one single fundamental content*, to express its surpassing richness and at the same time to bring it close to man under different aspects" (no. 4). And in the note he adds, "In this way, we have inherited from the Old Testament – as it were in a special synthesis – not only the wealth of expressions used by those books in order to define God's mercy, but also a specific and obviously anthropomorphic "psychology" of God: the *image of His anxious love*, which in contact with evil, and in particular with the sin of the individual and of the people, *is manifested as mercy*" (note 52).

This humble, compassionate and long-suffering Father is also rich in hope and deeply merciful: he waits at the window for his son's return and does not hesitate to meet both sons and to welcome them to the feast of his love. He is a Father who goes out of himself to turn towards his creatures, making himself a pilgrim, a beggar for love's sake. When the elder son angrily refuses to join in the feast, "the father came out and began to plead with him" (Lk 15:28). A man who takes part in the story of his children with a passion as respectful as it is real and deeply felt is a liberating Father who desires that all should be his guests at the feast. His joy springs from the fact that this child "was dead and has come to life", namely has found himself and the truth of his being, "was lost and has been found," namely, has returned to his father's house.

This is how the God of Israel loves his chosen people, with a passionate love that makes him share their joys and sorrows, and makes him desire the good of his beloved, who is, albeit secondarily, the joy of his fatherly heart. "My people are bent on turning away from me. To the Most High they call, but he does not raise them up at all. How can I give you up, Ephraim? How can I hand you over, O Israel? ... My heart recoils within me; my compassion grows warm and tender" (Hos 11:7-8).

What does all this have to say to us? Above all it

says that for us as Christians the first mirror in which we can learn to see the Father's face is the Hebrew Bible, received by our Church in humble gratitude as its first sacred book. By praying and meditating with the Bible we can journey together toward the Father of all.

In second place it tells us that we must feel tremendous sorrow for the tragedies that throughout history have befallen the Jews, the Father's beloved people, which culminated in the attempt during the last World War to destroy them utterly (the Shoah). We must humbly confess our complicity and reject any form of anti-Semitism (cf the document of the *Commission for Religious Relations with the Jews – We Remember: a Reflection on the Shoah*, 1998).

In third place, we must read in the history of the Jewish people the continuous presence of God's mysterious face both up to today and in the future. God loves these his children today as ever, in faithfulness to the Covenant made with them and which will never be revoked. Through them he makes his name blessed in every corner of the Earth, and God still calls them today. Even though not everyone has responded yet, as it has been given to us to do, in this expectancy there is a mystery that will be revealed in the future. We await, with them, the moment when all hearts will be opened.

In the fourth place it tells us that we are called by Jesus to contemplate in the Father of Israel his own Father, the Father of Humanity, he who wants us to be children in the Son.

5. Abba, the Father of Jesus

There is a crucial difference between the faith of Israel and what Jesus reveals to us of his Father, namely that he, the Nazarene, is the eternal Son, that he makes us one with himself and that he teaches us to be children. No-one can be truly a "child" if not in him. No "rejection of the Father" can be overcome except by entering into Jesus.

Jesus makes us sharers in his own sonship. This is why he put the *Our Father*, the children's prayer, on our lips, and gives us the Spirit who cries out in us the word that expresses filial love better than any other: "Abba! Father" (cf Rom 8:15 and Gal 4:6). The Christian's understanding of the Father's mystery cannot be voiced in words, but is rooted in Jesus Christ the Son's understanding of it, and it is entrusted to the grace of the Holy Spirit. This mystery of the Father goes beyond any thought or idea, and cannot be contained in words – it is always "beyond". Nevertheless, we grasp so much of it just from the word Jesus used – Abba!

Jesus also speaks this word during the agony in the garden, as the hour of his supreme self-offering on the cross approaches. "They went to a place called Gethsemane; and he said to his disciples, 'Sit here while I pray.' He took with him Peter and James and John, and began to be distressed and agitated. And said to them, 'I am deeply grieved, even to death; remain here, and keep awake.' And going a little farther, he threw himself on the ground and prayed that, if it were possible, the hour might pass from him. He said, 'Abba, Father, for you all things are possible; remove this cup from me; yet, not what I want, but what you want.'" (Mk 14:32-36).

In his terrible agony Jesus teaches us to be children. He does this especially by taking upon himself the anxiety that the human heart feels when faced by death. Jesus does not hurl this pain back in the Father's face, as if to blame him for giving him the life which now hurtles towards the abyss. The Father is not an adversary to shower our angry refusals upon; rather he is a confidant to whom we can entrust our final prayer, trusting utterly in his plans for us, however dark and mysterious they may seem. The word of confidence and tenderness, the name "Abba!" used by the Jews to express in a homely way the relationship of trust in one's earthly father, becomes here the expression of the sonship lived by Jesus and in which through him we share, far beyond our own limitations.

He entrusts himself to God, even when it seems he has been totally abandoned by him. He places himself in the Father's hands even when darkness covers the Earth and the veil of the Temple is torn in two. "Father, into your hands I commend my spirit" (Lk 23:46). These are the words of Psalm 31:6, which again highlights the continuity between the person of the Father Jesus turns to and the Father of Israelite faith. Moreover, the fact that it is he who pronounces these words, the only Son who became human, gives them a new flavour and a new power.

Thanks to the Son, we too can make those words our own and transform our fear into a trusting abandon, our rebellion into a liberating consignment of self. Jesus lived in the fear and darkness of death so that we might be able to live our life and death in self-abandonment to a faithful God. The Father who seems to forsake us, as he forsook his Son, "My God, my God, why have you forsaken me?" (Mk 15:34), in fact accepts our self-abandonment just as he accepts that of the dying crucified One who was handed over for our sake.

The good news announced by the Cross is that the Son has shared profoundly in our mortality, our weakness and fear, and that we are now children in the Son, and have a Father in heaven who will never stop loving his pilgrim children with a faithful tenderness as they journey towards him.

The discovery of God as Father happens in Jesus Christ. Only he can reveal it to us in fullness. The discovery brings us to think of, and experience, God not only as the Most High Lord and Master, but *at the same time* as welcoming, kind, attentive to my every footstep, accessible, provident and forgiving. To say Father in no way detracts from the meaning of other words like God and Lord, and all they signify of creative power, first beginning and final end that they signify. Rather it lends these attributes a connotation of benevolence, care, pardon, perseverance in love and so forth.

6. The Father of the disciples, "Our Father"

So, we are children in the Son and we can thus pray to God as to a father – "When you pray, say 'Father'" (Lk 11:2).

At this point it would be good to explain the

prayer of the *Our Father* in preparation for the gift we will make of it during the Christmas pastoral visitations (cf *Working Together 1998/99**, p. 8). For this event there is a study guide in preparation (*ibid.*, p. 9) and I will speak of it myself during the Lenten catecheses (*ibid.*, p. 11). Here I will limit myself to three points: (a) the words of the prayer; (b) in particular the prayer for forgiveness; (c) the effects of this prayer on our human experience.

a. When Jesus teaches the disciples to pray, he reveals to them how deeply he has made them sharers in his sonship. Even though he makes a distinction between himself and his own, "You should pray in this way" (Mt 6:9), Jesus gives his own Father to be their Father and has filled them with the Spirit that cries out in them Son's word – Abba! We say all the words of the *Our Father* with this spirit of sonship, and in turn this prayer reveals to us our condition as children in the Son.

This Father is "in heaven", distinct from any earthly father (cf Mt 23:9), and is the loving, first beginning of everything, waiting for us, to offer us an everlasting embrace at life's fulfilment.

Bearing in mind the Semitic turns of phrase ("the divine passive"), the first three invocations of the *Our Father* ask that God himself act (in other words "May your name be held holy" means "Sanctify your name in our midst!"). The disciples are such not on account of their own merits and efforts, but because they have received this free gift, so that

* This document, *Lavorare insieme 1998/99*, is at present available only in Italian.

in them "God's name is made holy, God's reign is brought forth, and his will is realised on Earth". In this sense, as St John makes plain, each one of the disciples, before becoming one who loves, is "the beloved" – "In this is love, not that we loved God but that he loved us and sent his Son to be the atoning sacrifice for our sins." (1 Jn 4:10)

Knowing that we are so loved we can pray: "Give us each day our daily bread", that is, feed and sustain us in the midst of every day's pressing needs, both spiritual and bodily, and welcome us as we are, with all our fragility. "Forgive us our sins, as we ourselves forgive those who are indebted to us", that is, forgive all our faults and enable us to forgive those who have offended us; help us to make fraternal relationships with everyone, rooted in a joyful relationship with you. "Do not bring us into temptation, but rescue us from evil" – may Satan, our enemy who tries to separate us from you, never triumph over us; sustain us in the time of testing so that, together with the Eternal Son, we may call upon you as a tender and faithful "Abba" and always be ready to do not our will but yours.

b. The request "forgive us our sins" should be particularly deepened throughout 1999. In fact the Pope has asked that in the third year of preparation for the millennium there be a special effort towards conversion and reconciliation, and hopes the sacrament of penance will be rediscovered. For this reason the Lombard Dioceses have published a supplement called *The Way of Conversion and the Sacrament of Penance: Pastoral Guidelines and a Map of the Penitential Churches* (1998). We recommend this text to those who wish to go deeper into this aspect of the pre-millennial year. "Father, forgive us our sins" will be our Lenten theme in 1999 (cf *Working Together 1998/99*, pp. 9-13).

The request for the forgiveness of sins is linked to forgiveness of our brothers and sisters: "Forgive us our sins, as we ourselves forgive those who are indebted to us". Jesus talks of forgiving "seventy times seven" (Mt 18:22). Whom do we forgive? All those from whom we think we have received some injury, some maltreatment; all those who have been a disappointment to us, who have withheld love, attention or a listening ear from us when we felt we needed it. We bear so many small hurts and bitternesses that are in need of the ointment and balm of continual and sincere forgiveness. That will make us feel better, healthier even, and give us a taste of the Father's forgiveness, not only for our sins, but for our shortcomings, for everything we have denied to God that he could have expected from us in faith and love, for all our many sins of omission.

In the light of the Father's revelation expressed in the words of the *Our Father* the life of a disciple is, like any other kind of human life, a pilgrimage, but a pilgrimage of returning home, of conversion to a love that forgives and that heals the soul's injuries and history's wounds. A disciple lives in a state of continual conversion, caught up in an ever deeper experience of being loved by God the Father in Jesus the Son. Docile to the workings of the Spirit, the disciple enters ever more deeply into God, hidden with Christ in the Father's heart (cf

Col 3:3). Herein lies the joy, the freedom and peace of being a disciple; this is where we feel the strength of being a new creature and irradiating the newness of life in all our being.

Let us ask ourselves: when we pray the *Our Father*, do we feel something of this peace and joy and fullness? Why not try occasionally praying the *Our Father* not in a minute but perhaps taking half an hour, enjoying and digesting each word? Why not, like St Teresa, take even longer over just the word Father? Silence will say more to us than many words.

The many young people from Europe who come to Milan after Christmas for the "Taizé prayer" (cf *Working Together 1998/99*, p. 9 no. 3) will teach us something of this prayer. We thank them even now for the help they will give us in entering into ourselves to worship the Father in silence (cf Mt 6:6).

c. Once more, let us ask ourselves: what does all this we have said about God's revelation as Father have to say to us about being a father or mother on Earth? If at the end of the first part we remembered that mistaken conceptions of God's fatherhood can result from distorted relationships within the family, the opposite is also true. Happy experiences of family life (and spiritual and pastoral paternity) predispose us to grasp from the words of faith the mystery of our loving relationship with the One to whom we owe everything. There is therefore a great burden of responsibility on Christian parents. Children learn to look at their Father in heaven from their parents' way of living and praying. Parents (and, by association, all those who have a role within the Church) will find light and comfort in their task, which cannot be delegated, by reciting the *Our Father* and meditating on the way in which God shows himself to be a Father.

From this prayer, repeated in every Eucharist, the Church is continually regenerated as a community of love and forgiveness. We feel ourselves forgiven by the Father in heaven and welcome one another with our own differences and weaknesses. A community that prays the *Our Father* is a community journeying unremittingly towards reconciliation, taking its inspiration from the Father's heart.

The Father's heart is our home and will be our eternal homeland. In this heart we discover our sonship and recognise that we are bound to all of those who, with us, make up the Church, in the brotherhood of mercy received and given. In the presence of the Father and his heart, the Church, though wounded by the sins of her children, is called to be, unceasingly and with renewed vigour, a family of loving disciples, wherein the first and all-embracing rule is charity, the *agapé* with which the Father has loved us and continually renews us in love.

The Father who welcomes us is also the Father who sends us out to others, as he sent and handed over his Son. In the Father's heart the disciple's life opens out towards dialogue and fraternal encounter with everyone, including those who seem so far away from experiencing the love of the Father of Jesus.

And so we move on to the third part of our letter.

Let us meet one another in the Father of us all!

7. With those who believe in God

The return to the Father of Jesus allows the disciples to discover a more universal brotherhood that unites them to every human person inasmuch as they are loved by the only Father. In particular we can see and experience this brotherhood with those who believe in some way in a mysterious divinity. They can live with their hearts open to the ultimate Mystery in the same way as the disciples of Jesus, and can entrust themselves in fear and trembling, and often with confidence as well, to the Transcendent one who is confessed and adored under different names and in different ways.

The prayer of the *Our Father* "Hallowed be your name" also includes, naturally, all those in whom God is glorified, independently of any visible membership in the community of Jesus' disciples. In fact there is in every human person a capacity for "self-transcendence", that is, an instinct placed deep within the heart by the Spirit that urges us to go out of ourselves in openness to an Other we can entrust ourselves to unreservedly. The ways of grace can therefore reach the hearts of everyone who is so disposed, even those that through no fault of their own do not recognise Christ as their only Saviour.

This has prompted some to go as far as defining as "anonymous Christians" those who, although outside Christianity, intently seek God, or at any rate an "ultimate reality". Attractive as it sounds, this concept runs the risk of overstretching the truth of the situation by attributing to those who believe in God, but not in Jesus, an orientation they themselves would expressly deny. We must avoid making a theoretical analysis of the workings of the human heart that oversimplifies the variety and complexity of the historical situation in which every individual finds him or herself.

Without wishing to put a Christian label on anyone, however, we still have to ask: if we start from the attraction we all feel towards the Mystery, is it possible to establish an authentic dialogue between Jesus' disciples and those who believe in God but do not recognise Jesus as the only Saviour of the world? The question also responds to a clear pastoral need within the Church, bearing in mind that the mass migrations of recent years have brought more and more people to live among us who profess other faiths, often rooted in centuries and centuries of history, culture and spiritual experience that are quite different from our own.

We should ask ourselves:

a. How can we engage these people in dialogue without losing a sense of Christ's primacy and the urgent need to witness to him?

b. What spiritual benefits can we share with each other even when there are basic differences between us in terms of our religious choices?

a. The knowledge of the sole Father of all revealed in Jesus can help us in our search for a right response to the question of dialogue and inter-religious meetings. If the Father is unique, the entire human community can be conceived as a single family where each one of us is called to walk a long path of conversion towards the Father, in order to recognise himself or herself as a child of equal dignity and equal rights before the universal Father of all brothers and sisters. The trusting self-abandonment to the divine mystery, a respectful attitude towards everyone and the willingness to embark upon the journey towards our common Father seem to me to be three very important points of contact. They are the basis on which we can establish sincere relationships of collaboration and friendship.

Such a style of fraternity and dialogue in no way means renouncing our witness of the one who revealed the Father's face to us and taught and handed on to us the experience of being a child of God. No inter-religious dialogue would be authentic if it implied any renunciation of our Christian identity and especially our confession of the name of Jesus. To live as one of his disciples, however, means learning more and more to be children and to help others be children with him and in him. This is why the confession of the Saviour Son in no way conflicts with the recognition of a broader fraternity. Indeed it helps us offer everyone a way to sustain and enrich the path we are all walking on our journey towards the Other, whom we can entrust ourselves to unreservedly.

To live as a disciple of Jesus means, in particular, living the Sermon on the Mount (Mt 5-7), based upon the Beatitudes (Mt 5:3-17). This is what the Christian is asked to do and teach (cf Mt 28:20). It is a lifestyle that excludes no-one and rejects no-one but on the contrary attracts people on account of its undeniable moral beauty. To be poor in spirit, pure in heart, merciful, ready to forgive, pray for enemies and so forth means to offer the way of Christ to everyone, giving worth to all that is deepest and truest in every Christian soul and every religion.

This attitude excludes any form of proselytism that denies value in others' faith, and the relativism, or rather misunderstood pluralism, that equates one subjectively achieved truth with any another. Disciples of Jesus cannot but keep a critical watch over themselves, their community and especially over any other experience of the divine, because they know well how many spurious elements can insinuate themselves into their relationship with the Father. This can be in the form of conflict and rejection, or uncalled for projections of human desire and calculation onto the face of God. Calm dialogue, interwoven with mutual listening and generous and careful discernment can help disciples live out an authentic experience of the Holy Spirit in their encounters with other believers. The Spirit is the bond of unity between the disparate and helps each of us cry out a heartfelt and lively "Abba!" to the only Father of all.

This demands that inter-religious dialogue be conducted in faithfulness to our own beliefs and in honesty of heart, so as to hear the other without prejudice or a closed mind, ready to accept all they offer us that is good, with the freedom to suggest the newness of the Gospel that reveals God the universal Father's face and heart through the royal road that is Jesus. There are some practical suggestions on this matter in *Working Together 1998/99* (pp. 15-16) under the heading "Some examples of dialogue and discernment".

b. We should also ask ourselves how we can make a mutual exchange of spiritual goods with other believers in God who follow other religions.

Jesus' return to the Father allows the disciples to discover a more universal brotherhood and sisterhood that unites them with every other human creature inasmuch as they are loved by the sole Father and destined to be with him. God, the sole creator of all that exists, of all things visible and invisible, is also the loving Father of all his creatures, who calls them to respect the whole of creation with the feelings of "reverence", as St Ignatius of Loyola puts it, they owe the Creator himself.

From the shared recognition of the responsibility we owe before God our Lord and Father to every creature, springs a common commitment to care for the dignity of every person, human fraternity, justice and peace, in the other great religions there is also a longing for compassion and a hunger for justice, together with the total rejection of violence and a common seeking after ways to secure these goals for the whole of humanity.

Moreover, God's fatherhood – as the expression of the bond between all that exists and the holy

Mystery that has called everything into existence and maintains it – is the basis of a real need for loving attentiveness towards the great house of the world that bears in every creature an impression of the Creator's loving footstep. The sense of divine fatherhood is thus joined to a so-called "ecological" awareness; it unites all of humanity's great religions in their original message, namely that they all have a common respect for creation.

Faced with the tremendous violence that can and has been visited upon the natural world, our age is called upon to rediscover this awareness. God the Father and Creator calls everyone who recognises him as such to prevent the growing inequality between biological and historical time, that is, the growing divide between the slow rate of natural growth and the frantic speed of human demands and activity. This divide is the basis of the "ecological crisis" that is in evidence across the planet, in the devastating effects of nuclear technology or atmospheric pollution, for example. On a personal level, the crisis is evinced in the extremely delicate field of biomedical research.

8. With those who do not believe (those who are searching and the indifferent)

If the relationship with the Father of all allows us to have a profound encounter with those who believe in God and are therefore open to the Mystery revealed in love by the Father-Mother, it is of no less assistance in our dialogue with those who do not believe but are open to the discovery of the hidden Face.

We disciples live out our relationship with the Father as an unceasing pilgrimage towards him, a kind of homecoming that is never completely finished. In this sense, those who believe in God the father know they must continually turn towards him, overcoming the fears, worries and interior conflicts they are constantly faced with, and that often come from the culture they live in.

The believer is in some way a non-believer who struggles each day to begin believing again, a child who must continually overcome himself or herself and offer himself or herself into God's hands in an attitude of filial obedience and unconditional self-surrender. If it weren't like that, faith would be an ideology, the presumption of having understood everything, rather than the constant returning and renewed self-abandonment to the Other who welcomes us in loving trust.

We disciples can recognise part of ourselves in the thinking unbeliever, who suffers as a result of God's absence from his or her heart, and lives in an anxious seeking. Perhaps this is the part that urges us most strongly to search in the Father for the door of salvation and the peace we long for. A profound and inward encounter then becomes possible between believers and unbelievers in their shared seeking, ready to bear the weight of honest questioning. Each listens to the other and finds therein something of his or her own self, and can cleanse himself or herself by learning from the disquiet lived by the other and from the light that sparkles in his or her anxious heart.

This encounter demands our intellectual honesty,

courage and unremitting love of truth, and must deliberately shun both the easy recourse to slogans, to ready-made labels and to entrenched and non-negotiable positions, as well as to a superficial seeking after peace that tries at all costs to find points of contact even when they cannot stand up to attentive and sincere examination.

In reality the Father is drawing everyone to himself, but in different ways and at different speeds that we must learn to recognise and respect. Faith is a encounter mysterious in its whys and wherefores. Jesus' question, "When the Son of Man comes, will he find faith on the earth?" (Lk 18:8) serves to disabuse believers of any presumption that they are more successful or better than anyone else. Our faith is always at risk and needs to be constantly fed by a love that listens and prays and feeds the heart and keeps it turned towards the Father.

It is precisely in this way that dialogue with non-believers can prompt us as disciples to be watchful in our faith and make us humbler and active in our questioning before him to whom we entrust ourselves. "I believe, help my unbelief" (Mk 9:24) is indeed the prayer of everyone who is searching for meaning in their life.

What about those who are indifferent, and the unbeliever who flees from any questions about the ultimate Mystery, perhaps lounging in the mire of warm feelings offered by some of the new esoteric cults that ask none of the important existential questions? How can we disciples of the Son meet those whose unbelief is a result of indifference to the only Father?

We must say straightaway that the superficial, unthinking atheist is not that much different from the believer who refuses to think or enter into serious debate with God. In reality the certainty that guides their hearts and minds is bought cheaply, deliberately gratuitous and not thought through. To believe or not to believe in God for the sake of personal ease or to avoid being disturbed are similar to one another when considered as a way of being in the Father's presence. We are once more faced by the "two sons" of the parable of Lk 15.

Disciples of Jesus should therefore especially examine themselves in order to guard against running, or having run in vain, freeing themselves from the spiritual laziness that leads to them avoid honest questions and take refuge in evasive consolations. When we do this, in order to live out our relationship with the Father as a "devouring fire" that feeds every day upon the Word and prayer, we can approach superficial atheists with the humble power of our questioning. Rather than giving answers, we will stimulate in them hidden or buried questions, in such a way that their own hearts will begin to move towards the Mystery.

A believer's authentic witness is a kind of scandal, a stumbling block that makes people think. It does not mean offering facile certainties, or asking questions that fail to get to the heart of the matter, but it is rather at one and the same time a respectful yet disquietening presence, and "importunate friend", which challenges people to stir themselves and listen to the questionings of the unquiet heart that all children of the only Father have within themselves.

In this act of giving witness, every disciple has to be himself or herself, without demanding startling results and without feeling we have been sent to do things we aren't capable of. In humility and love, we all of us sow how and where we can, certain that the Father acts in our hearts first, drawing us all to himself in the Holy Spirit, and that he gives sweetness to everyone in their accepting and believing the truths, if we refuse to indulge in the excuses and defences with which our human wills can oppose the divine action.

In this way the invocation of the Father in respect of the coming of the Kingdom is also realised in the lives of believers and in their dealings with unbelievers. As we read in a minor manuscript tradition of Lk 11:3 regarding the gift of the Spirit that realises God's lordship in our hearts: "May your Holy Spirit come upon us and sanctify us".

See the suggestions on pages 7-8 of *Working Together 1998/99*, "the kerygmatic proclamation to those who are far away" and on pages 14-16, "Proclamation and dialogue in the ecclesial mystery" for some practical instances of dialogue with unbelievers.

Finally, we must not forget the co-operation that goes on for the good of humanity with those who also uphold important values on important ethical matters, even when they do not know how to trace them to their fundamental origin. Some of these ideas have already been mentioned when we were discussing co-operation with the great religions: justice, peace, and the stewardship of creation. We might also remember some other general themes which could form the basis for common reflection and action, for instance: human life as an inviolable mystery; the dignity of the human person and the care for the lowest in our society (see the following section); the family as the fundamental unit of society viewed as a community of love, a way towards the life and education of future generations, and a way of hope and solidarity.

9. With the poor

Jesus' Father is the Father of the poor, not simply because Jesus wanted to be poor and declared that "Blessed are the poor in spirit. Theirs is the Kingdom of Heaven" (Mt 5:3), but also because only those who are poor in heart can be open to unconditional self-offering. Certainly, poverty is not an instant qualification for meeting God the Father. When poverty is a lack of material or spiritual goods it can be the cause of rebellion against the Father. This kind of poverty – which it would be better to call "indigence" – is contrary to the Father's will, who feeds the birds of the air and clothes the lilies of the field and does not want any of his creatures to be without what they need (cf Mt 6:25ff).

The relationship between the disciple and the Father demands a twofold attitude to poverty. On the one hand, poverty of spirit, an openness and self-abandonment to the Father's providence, is necessary for an authentic experience of the merciful love of Jesus' God. On the other hand, as disciples we must do all we can to prevent indigent poverty from offending the Father's image in any of his children.

For those who believe in him, the return to the Father therefore means, together with conversion of heart, a serious and intent commitment to create the conditions necessary for all to enjoy their dignity in a way that no-one be denied the minimum conditions for recognising and worshipping the Father in Spirit and in truth.

The preferential option for the least among us, which the Church has professed in our days many times and in various contexts, does not distract us from the one thing necessary, which is the glorification of the Father. It is a way of realising in time our unconditional obedience to God the Father of all. In this sense we can understand the urgency many Christians feel in denouncing those situations in which the dignity of the human person is trodden underfoot and offended on account of injustice, indigence or by demands that seem unrealisable in the concrete situation the poor find themselves in. This is the invitation made by the Holy Father in *Tertio Millennio Adveniente*, to consider a "serious reduction", if not a "complete remission" of the international debts of the poorest countries, "which weigh down many nations" (no. 51). On this theme, see *Working Together 1998/99* (p. 13, no. 4).

However, it is not only in international relations that the return to the Father obliges believers to promote justice and human development. Our day-to-day relationships must also be touched by the need to see others as children of the same Father, brothers and sisters in humanity and grace.

I would like in particular to refer to the need to overcome any closed, egotistical thinking, in which we consider it necessary to defend our rights against the incursions of those whose needs are greater than our own. The greatness of any society is measured by its capacity to welcome, and share its resources with, those who need them. The acceptance of immigrants, within the confines of the law, is one of the ways we can recognise everybody's equal dignity before the only God, in the same way as showing solidarity with the weakest and most forgotten of our complex society. The refusal to make exceptions and the rejection of discriminatory mentalities is equally a fruit of the our recognition of the Father of all. We must not hesitate in recognising the risk that these attitudes which poison our culture leave us open to, namely of falling into grave sins of selfishness and blasphemy against God the Father.

The call to redouble our efforts in promoting charity and justice, and to overcome every kind of sectarianism and racism, flow from the prayer of the *Our Father* that asks that the will of the Father be done on Earth as it is in heaven. God wants all of us to be equal in dignity before him, brothers and sisters in accord with our material possibilities, but also through sharing in the common actions that lead to him. The Father of the poor helps us to look on the needs of others with an open heart and perceive in them (especially in the needs of the most deprived) the fundamental rights of the human person that no-one may overlook or ignore.

Christian brotherhood and sisterhood is more than a vague feeling or spiritual reality with no consequences for the way people live their lives. As the description in the Acts of the Apostles of the first community makes clear, the proclamation of the good news of God the Father is the basis of a new way of living that overcomes isolation and strives to calm conflict, creating conditions that favour the dignity and development of all people in accord with God's designs.

In praise of the Father:
the image of Mary

The many personal and communal demands placed upon us by the Father's return and the consequences of it and shows us how "the jubilee, centred on the figure of Christ," can and must become a "great act of praise to the Father" (John Paul II, *Tertio Millennio Adveniente*, no. 49), a "blessing" – proclaimed in word and made real in our lives – of the One who is Father of all. The task we are all called to is that of celebrating God's primacy just as he taught us, and he gave us the eternal Son made flesh to do the same. We are reminded of this in the hymn which opens the letter to the Ephesians (cf Eph 1:3-14).

Blessed be the God and Father of our
Lord Jesus Christ,
who has blessed us in Christ with every
spiritual blessing in the heavenly places.

The deep meaning of this tremendous blessing, an act of praise and thanksgiving, is the mysterious choice that means we have been called to share in the life of the Son in accord with an eternal plan that is over us and surrounds us.

He chose us in Christ before the foundation
of the world

to be holy and blameless before him in love.
He destined us for adoption as his children
    through Jesus Christ,
according to the good pleasure of his will.

This plan is the "mystery" which like a womb and a
shield, embraces the workings of the world and of
history entirely, making us perceive our solidarity
with and our sharing in the fate of the whole
universe.

With all wisdom and insight he has made
    known to us the mystery of his will,
according to his good pleasure that he set forth
    in Christ,
as a plan for the fullness of time, to gather up
    all things in him,
things in heaven and things on earth.

In particular, to be heirs of the Kingdom as children
made such in the Son, on the one hand fills us with
wonder and praise, and on the other commits us to
share with others the gift we have received.

In Christ we have also obtained an
    inheritance,
having been destined according to the purpose
    of him
who accomplishes all things according to
    his counsel and will,
so that we, who were the first to set our hope
    on Christ,
might live for the praise of his glory.
In him you also, when you had heard the word of

truth, the gospel of your salvation,
and had believed in him, were marked with the seal
of the promised Holy Spirit;
this is the pledge of our inheritance toward
redemption as God's own people,
to the praise of his glory.

To have received the gift of welcoming the Father's revelation and to become children in the Son is not a privilege but a task that urges us to recognise ourselves as united children of the only Father, and also to enter into dialogue with all people in truth, beginning with those who believe in God and ending with those who do not believe, and with all the poor whose dignity as children of God is trodden underfoot.

The task is so great that we feel almost crushed by it. The image of self-abandonment to the Father and of a life spent in praise of him that comforts us is that of the Virgin Mary (cf John Paul II, *Tertio Millennio Adveniente*, no. 54).

Just as she glorifies God the Father's marvellous works and sings of the deeds the Lord will effect in the lives of his children, we too with help of her motherly intercession can hope to be sharers in God's works and in bringing his joy to the hearts of our brothers and sisters. May the Spirit who was at work in Mary – daughter of the Father – and who made her the mother of the Son for the salvation of all, work also in us that we might live in fullness our vocation as children in the Son before the only Father, together with all who call upon him – using whatever name – or who are called to acclaim him as the only Lord, the God and Father of all.

Appendix

Some questions for a review of life, both personal and communal

1. Examination of our image of God

• What image do I have of God the Father? Is my God the God of Jesus? Do I trust myself utterly to him, placing my anxieties and fears into his hands?

• What face of God is presented in our catechesis and preaching? Is it that of God the Father of Jesus?

• Whether or not you feel that God is a Father, and experience him as your Father and the Father of everyone, is something that can be put to the proof, by the use of certain indicators. For example: do you feel genuine thankfullness for all that happens to you? Do you feel able to overcome the anguish or fatigue caused by the things that loom over you, without loosing touch with the reality of the situation? Are you capable of bearing injustice without giving in to constant recriminations in your heart, justifying and defending yourself? Are you able to say 'I trust in the steadfast love of God for ever and ever' (Ps 52:10).

2. Examination of our relationship with the secular world

• Am I a negligent or a thoughtful believer? In what way do I listen to the non-believer who is both inside me and beside me? Do I respect the searching of those who do not believe? Do I encourage them with my witness?

3. Examination of our relationship with those who believe in God

• What sort of relationship do I have with the faith of Israel, holy root of my own Christian existence? What is my relationship with the people of the Covenant which has never been revoked, the Jews?

• How do I live out my ecumenical commitment of dialogue and service, aimed at constructing that unity for which Jesus prayed? How is this commitment lived out at the community level in my Parish, at deanery level and in movements and associations?

• What welcome do I/we reserve for the believers of other religions? Is there dialogue? Is there co-operation particularly in the areas of justice, peace and the safeguarding of creation?

4. Examination of our relationship with the poor

• How do I/we live the fraternity that comes from the recognising of ourselves as children of the one

Father? In particular, how do we welcome the poorest of the poor and what do we do to express our solidarity with them? What notice do we take, individually and in our communities, of the poor of the earth, especially in situations of subordination, violence and hunger?

5. Examination of our contribution to the mission

• How does my faith in God the Father shine through in my words and in my life? How does this happen in our communities? Am I able to say to whoever does not know the God of Jesus, 'Come and see?'

• How do we support the mission to those peoples who still do not know the God of Jesus?